MONTESSORI AT HOME

A Complete Guide to Teaching
Your Preschooler at Home
Using the Montessori Method
Revised and Expanded

Heidi Anne Spietz

American Montessori Consulting
Rossmoor, California

ABOUT THE AUTHOR

Heidi Anne Spietz, author of "Montessori at Home" holds a B.Sc. degree from REX University of N.Y., Albany and a diploma in Montessori training. She is listed in the 1988 edition of Who's Who in American Education and in 1979 she was awarded, but declined because of other commitments, the prestigious CORO award. She holds general memberships in both the American Montessori Society and Association Montessori Internationale, Netherlands Chapter. She is well acquainted with how the Montessori method is used in the United States and in Europe, because she received her training from London, England. She has taught at private schools in the U.S. while concurrently managing her own successful tutoring business for the past seven years.

Library of Congress Cataloging-in-Publication Data

Spietz, Heidi Anne,
        Montessori at home : a complete guide to teaching your preschooler at home using the Montessori method / Heidi Anne Spietz. — Rev. and expanded.
            p.   cm.
        Includes bibliographical references (p.   ) and index.
        ISBN 0-929487-37-0 : $9.95
        1. Montessori method of education.   2. Home schooling. 3. Education, Preschool—Parent participation. I. Title.
    LB775.M8S76 1991
    649'.68—dc20
                                            91-18212
                                               CIP

TABLE OF CONTENTS

This book is dedicated to my family members Carl, Frances and Susan. I thank them for their encouragement and love.

CHAPTER 1
An Alternative Approach
To Learning

Maria Montessori, a prolific lecturer and writer, revolutionized the field of education. In time, her iconoclastic ideas about education spread to all continents of the world. Montessori's philosophy has not only been embraced by educators in the United States and the United Kingdom but also by educators in Africa, Sweden and the Netherlands, to name a few.

Maria was born in 1870 in the province of Ancona in Italy. Her parents were far from ordinary. Maria's father, a brilliant mathematician, was of nobility. Her mother, Renilde Stoppani, was the niece of Antonio Stoppani, a well recognized scientist. Consequently, Maria was encouraged by both parents to develop her mind and to consider a career in teaching. However, Maria shared her father's love for mathematics and she was intent on pursuing a career other than teaching.

After some consideration, Maria thought that she wanted to pursue a career in engineering. However, because she excelled in many subjects, numerous career possibilities were open to her. The field of medicine fascinated Maria, and she felt for a time that a career as a doctor would prove rewarding.

She worked hard in medical school. However, once she became a physician she found that her career in medicine was actually a stepping stone to something even far more rewarding.

Maria worked at the Orthophrenic Clinic in Rome, Italy. There she was assigned to work with children thought to be mentally impaired. Maria had studied writings by eminent scientists such as Seguin and Itard, and she had been inspired by their ideas. Ultimately, these ideas influenced her thinking about how to educate children.

Because of her unique role as a doctor she not only understood the psychological impacts of the environment on children but she understood the physiological and developmental impacts as well. She knew each of the developmental stages that a child goes through. She was aware of how a deprived environment might ultimately stunt proper development. She was also aware of how inadequate nutrition could affect the physiological and developmental processes needed for proper growth.

Thus, Dr. Maria Montessori devised a didactic method which included a set of materials to be used by any child. The first application of these materials used to help children labeled mentally deficient proved quite successful. Later she decided to use them to help other children learn.

THE TYPICAL MONTESSORI CLASSROOM

Montessori prepared an environment that was conducive to learning. She was sensitive to the needs of children. She realized that if these needs were met, the children would feel more relaxed. Thus, their "will" or "undivided attention" would be focused upon learning.

First, Dr. Montessori was perceptive enough to realize that the surroundings should fit the child. She obtained chairs and tables that were just the right size for the children.

These chairs and tables were light enough so that they could easily be moved by the children. She knew that children would not necessarily be impressed by the design of the furniture. Rather, they would be more impressed with being able to exert some control in their environment.

Montessori realized that children can easily manipulate furniture that is sized proportionately for the little ones. Thus, some of the initial lessons in a typical Montessori classroom center around moving chairs and tables in a quiet manner, so as not to disturb others. In a short time, the children learn how to properly pick up a chair, carry a chair and set it down again quietly. The child repeats this exercise many times, each time feeling a little more confident in his accomplishment.

Montessori realized that children need to repeat an exercise, and that it is imperative that we, as adults, respect the child's need to do this. Thus, Montessori gave the children ample time in which to repeat the exercises and to work with the Montessori apparatus. Because the children did not feel pressured, they became enthusiastic participants.

Montessori was also aware of how children make discoveries on their own. She knew that they needed to explore and manipulate their environment. Within the child there is an "inner teacher" which guides him. Therefore, a teacher's role is not to teach. Rather, the teacher's function is to provide a "prepared environment" for the child. This environment contains all of the elements needed for the child to make progress towards becoming a self-actualized human being.

A Montessori teacher presents one by one all of the exercises and apparatus to the child. Once the teacher is satisfied that the child understands the principles underlying each of the exercises she then removes herself and quietly observes the child from a distance. She gives the child much opportunity to repeat the exercise before attempting to present the next exercise. She encourages the child to strive towards perfection; however, she recognizes every small accomplishment by verbalizing her approval. She is always encouraging and patient.

The teacher acts as a companion and a confidant. She serves as a helper rather than a dictator. The Montessori teacher has been taught to demonstrate a genuine love and deep respect for the child. Because she knows that children are often more perceptive than adults, and thus can easily detect inflections in the human voice that denote sarcasm, terseness, etc., the teacher is careful about how she speaks to the child. The tone of her voice is neither condescending or didactic.

The Montessori schools of today are typically in a home setting. Each Montessori administrator selects an atmosphere that he or she feels will provide a "prepared" environment which will best serve the child.

In a typical Montessori facility one room might be designated as the chapel. In this room appropriate sized chairs would be assembled in rows, and in the center of the room one might place a long strip of carpeting which would serve as the main aisle. The color of the carpeting would most likely be a deep wine red, thus creating a church-like effect.

In the front of this room designated as the chapel, one might see a wooden or bronze colored cross. Thus, when children enter the chapel their attention is immediately focused upon Christ. Consequently, their thoughts would be centered around learning more about him.

Preferably the drapes would be a deep wine color, and stained glass windows depicting religious scenes often provide a nice touch. However, stained glass windows are quite expensive and many school budgets probably would not permit such a lavish purchase. Therefore, as an alternative, children have the opportunity to participate in a fun stained glass art project. The children either paint or color large pieces of translucent paper where religious scenes have been outlined in black. (An additional stained glass project using translucent paper will be covered later in this book.)

If the teacher elects to have the children complete the stained glass windows project, she would discuss the significance of the various religious scenes. Then, the finished products could be placed on clear windows where the stained glass effect would be quite stunning.

On the walls you might notice pictures with a religious theme, e.g. Jesus, His disciples, among many others.

Art and music are an important means of expressing one's religion, and as we know, children love to sing hymns with the accompaniment of an organ or a piano. Therefore, you will often see a piano or an organ in a typical Montessori facility.

It is important to note, as this point, that some Montessori facilities may use Montessori's philosophy to teach the Jewish tradition. Moreover, many Montessori schools are secular, and thus the use of a chapel is absent in such schools. The diversity in these schools reflects the diversity apparent in the population of this great country.

If you are able to visit a Montessori facility you may also see a room set aside for the teaching of science. You will probably notice that the room selected is a room that receives a lot of sunlight. Here, the children learn much about nature. Each child learns about plants first-hand by assuming complete responsibility for the care of his plant.

On the walls in this room you might see colorful posters about science related subjects such as the different types of plants, the basic four groups of nutrition, rocks and minerals, or the different types of animals. It would not be unusual to see, one month, posters showing the different types of animals. The next month, perhaps, you might see posters showing how we select foods from the basic four food groups.

In a room comparable to a living room in the modern house, you would probably see the children busily engaging in the Montessori exercises. In one bookcase you might find the sensorial material used in reinforcing math concepts. In another bookcase you might see sensorial material used to reinforce reading and phonics concepts.

The administrator usually selects a decor that will be most conducive to a relaxed learning environment. Usually, the colors chosen are warm and cheerful. Warm autumn greens and rusts are often used in this room. The carpet chosen is a durable type, possibly brown in color, and most likely wall to wall. At one end of the room you might notice a sturdy but comfortable couch where a child is encouraged to rest whenever he feels the need to.

Many of the Practical Life Exercises are learned in a room that is most comparable a kitchen. In this room children learn how to wash their hands, wash fruit and so forth. Because the chairs and tables are small and can be easily manipulated, the children feel enthusiastic about learning these skills.

You will notice that all of the materials that the children use are placed in cupboards where the children can easily reach them. Thus, the children can be quite independent when they practice skills like setting the table, or washing the dishes.

At some of the Montessori facilities you will notice the movement of small animals about. You might see a small shed located outside near the main Montessori building. Children often keep animals like frogs, chickens and cats in such a shed. Children are taught how to care for these animals, thus receiving a lesson in responsibility.

CHAPTER II
Learning In A
Home Environment

From the moment of birth your child's quest for understanding begins. He not only learns about the environment around him but also about his relationship to the environment. He does this by listening, touching, seeing and by becoming a participant. Often, the parent provides the child with these needed experiences by taking him to places like a friend's house, the grocery store, or to the park. Thus, the parent's role in the child's development is crucial in determining how a child interacts with his environment.

If a child is not allowed to fully experience what his environment has to offer him, his development suffers. Conversely, if a child is encouraged to explore and manipulate objects in this environment, communicate his thoughts to others and demonstrate some independence, then he is well on his way to becoming a self-actualized human being. By providing your child with such an environment you are playing an integral part in your child's developmental process.

PRESENTING THE LESSONS TO YOUR CHILD

Montessori at Home is designed specifically for you, the parent. Included are step-by-step illustrations and pictures of the various Montessori exercises and Montessori apparatus as described in this book. Directions for using the apparatus, most of which can be made at home, will be found in the appropriate chapters in this book.

The exercises and apparatus presented will benefit children from three to five years of age. The exercises and apparatus should be presented to your child in a sequential manner. Do not skip any of the exercises, even if you feel that your child is ready for a more advanced exercise.

Select a specified time at least three times per week to work with your child or children. If you have two or more preschoolers that are in the three to five year age range then by all means encourage them to participate together. Do not let television programs, telephone calls, etc. interfere with this special time that you and your child or children share together.

Naturally, if illness causes you or your child to feel tired and irritable, you may want to skip a session. It is better to skip a session than to work with each other in a tense environment. Such an environment only breeds resentment at having to complete the exercises. Remember, you want the sessions to be productive and happy experiences for your child.

Select a room in your house or apartment that, in your opinion, will be most conducive to learning. This room, preferably, will be one where you would receive few if any interruptions or distractions. Remember, the environment should be as relaxed as possible. Never attempt to present your child with the Montessori exercises and apparatus with a television blasting away in the next room. Also, older siblings in the household need to realize that for one hour or so three times a week, you are unavailable to them except for an emergency.

Before you present any of the Montessori apparatus or exercises to your child, make certain that you have read the material thoroughly. If you have any questions about the material, read it a second time. Then practice doing the exercise or working with the Montessori apparatus yourself. You will be surprised what you learn from doing the exercises and working with the apparatus. You will gain invaluable insight which will be quite useful when you actually present the materials to your child. Because children are quite perceptive, your child will assimilate some of this knowledge and use it to help him better understand the concept that is being presented.

These exercises are designed to enhance development of the five senses as well as the mind. By doing exercises which heighten awareness of how things smell, taste, and so forth, the child becomes sensitive to the delightful smells that permeate the kitchen at dinner time. Further, he may notice the deep yellow bouquet of sunflowers that serves as a centerpiece on the dining room table. The child becomes acutely aware of what the world has to offer him, and he learns his relationship to this world.

If you plan to work with two or more of your children at the same time, you must be conscious of what this type of learning session may create. First, don't compare your children. Remember that each child is precious and relates to learning at a different rate. Never forget that each child is unique and has something special to offer. Second, while you are presenting the oldest with advanced material, be aware that your younger children may be interested too. Do not discourage this! In a typical Montessori school, the younger children often learn some of the concepts that are being presented to the older children.

Likewise, if your older child wishes to help, not boss, his little brother or sister, allow this. Your older child will gain self-confidence from the fact that he gave some assistance. This interaction is healthy because it gives practice in the needed skill of cooperation.

Third, don't criticize your child's efforts. Concentrate on each of his successes and allow him to see an expression of approval written on your face. If you constantly praise one child but not the other an unhealthy competition may arise.

Finally, each child should be encouraged to fully complete the exercises. By doing so, you are setting a pattern of completing tasks in life rather quitting when obstacles become apparent.

Even though you have introduced several exercises and presented several of the Montessori apparatus to your child, you may find that he or she only wants to work with one or two during your time together. This should not be discouraged.

Your child needs an ample amount of time to work with the material. He should not feel pressured. You must not make him feel rushed. If you approach each session with a positive attitude and remain calm and reassuring, you will be giving your child pleasurable learning experiences that he will remember throughout his life.

CHAPTER III
The Three Year Old's
Quest For Independence

During the first three years of your child's life you have seen a rapid succession of developmental processes at work. When your child was about 6 months of age he simply babbled. Now, at three years of age, his level of communication is actually quite sophisticated. He is able to verbalize his thoughts to you by using phrases.

Likewise, his coordination has improved. At 6 months he was able to sit up. By three years of age he is now able to run around the house and is quite eager to become an active participant in his environment. He has felt for some time that he was somewhat powerless and that his environment controlled him. However, now because of increased neuromuscular development, he is able to more fully interact with his environment.

MOVEMENT - YOUR THREE YEAR OLD'S KEY TO LEARNING

Movement is perhaps one of the most important components of learning. Your child intuitively realizes this. Thus, your three year old child is anxious to learn more about his environment by moving about. He wishes to be actively involved, not simply a passive observer.

Montessori realized the importance of movement in the child's development. Thus, she devoted much time discussing movement in many of her books. The titles of her books can be found on page 113 of this book.

Montessori incorporated movement with a child's need for independence when she devised the Practical Life Exercises. By completing these exercises a child gains confidence in his ability to function as a responsible human being. The exercises involve handling such things as chairs, tables, cups and saucers in a responsible manner.

Before you prepare to present these exercises to your child you will want to check to see if you have what is needed close at hand. For example, you may want to obtain child sized furniture for your child. If you have a relative who loves working with wood you might consider asking him to construct a small table and chairs(s) for your child.

If you would rather purchase such equipment you may want to contact some Used Furniture Stores. If you want to buy new furniture, you may want to contact Lakeshore Curriculum. The address can be found on page 116 of this book. You may also want to purchase child sized plastic drinking glasses, plastic cups and saucers, plastic plates, safety scissors, and a broom, to name a few. These items can be found in local toy stores, some department stores and by mail through Lakeshore Curriculum or ABC School Supply.

Now, take a moment to study an outline of some of the Practical Life Exercises.

A. Exercises in Elementary Body Movement
   1. Manipulating objects
      a. Teaching children to handle objects correctly
         1. plastic tray
         2. plastic drinking glasses
         3. plastic plates
         4. small boxes

2. Practice walking quietly
3. Pouring
    a. Water into a plastic container
    b. Rice into a plastic container

4. Opening and closing
    a. doors
    b. cupboards
    c. books
    d. boxes

5. Cutting with plastic safety scissors
    a. fabric
    b. paper
    c. ribbon

6. Sewing
    a. threading big plastic needle with yarn

7. Preparing food
    a. washing fruit
    b. drying fruit
    c. putting margarine/butter on bread, muffins, rolls, etc.
    d. slicing bread with plastic knife

Montessori felt that these exercises should be presented step by step.

Therefore, before you present an exercise to your child make sure that you have a well organized plan. It may help to write out the plan to see if you have left out any steps.

For example, when teaching your child to wash fruit, you, of course, will need a plastic plate, plastic bowl, fruit, sink, paper towel and a sponge. You will then present the exercise in the following manner:

PRESENTATION

1. Remove fruit from bin or basket
2. Grip/hold fruit in one hand
3. Carry fruit to sink or basin
4. Hold fruit in sink or basin with one hand
5. With the other hand turn on faucet
6. Then, remove hand from faucet
7. Pick up sponge with this hand
8. Turn fruit gently with one hand under stream of water
9. Now, in addition to movement #8, gently scrub exterior of fruit
10. Shut off faucet
11. Place sponge back in its original position
12. Pick up a paper towel
13. Lift fruit from the sink or basin

14. Gently wipe excess moisture from the fruit
15. Place fruit in bowl or on a plate
16. Discard paper towel in wastebasket

Initially, you will present the exercise to your child. Be sure that you don't rush through the exercise. Encourage your child to listen and watch closely. If your child has any questions after you have completed your presentation, repeat the presentation again. Then, let him try to complete the exercise. Refrain from criticizing his efforts even if he makes some mistakes. If he is anxious to repeat the exercise encourage him to do so. If you feel frustrated wait until another time and then encourage him to try again.

You may find that the Practical Life Exercises are presented in various manners in related Montessori books. However, I have chosen to present this next category second.

B. Caring for the Environment
    1. Learning to use a broom
        a. First, sweeping in a relatively small area
        b. Later, in larger area

    2. Washing the floor

3. Dusting
   a. with a rag cloth
   b. using a feather duster

4. Washing dishes

5. Care of a garden
   a. planting seeds
   b. watering
   c. weeding

6. Care of an animal

Once again, when you present exercises in this second category, keep in mind that you must give your child a step by step instruction as to what is expected of him. Carefully study the following presentation on feeding a cat. Notice how each step, however obvious to you, is presented. Remember, your child does not yet have the reasoning powers that you have.

PRESENTATION

1. Remove box of cat food from the shelf with both hands
2. Support the box with one hand held underneath
3. Carry the box over to where a clean cat's dish can be found (a small table will do)

4. Put the box of cat food on the table

5. Pick up the cat's clean dish

6. With one hand lift up the box

7. Place the other hand on the upper side of the bowl

8. Gently tilt the box so that food will pour out

9. Fill the dish halfway

10. Using both hands, carry the box back to the shelf

11. Place box back into its proper place

12. Walk back to table

13. Pick up dish and carefully carry it to area where cat eats

14. Gently place dish down on the floor

Social courtesies make life so much easier for your child. By practicing the next set of exercises your child can feel comfortable when socializing with others. For example, he will know what is expected of him in different social situations and thus feel confident and eager to participate.

C. Social Courtesies

1. Greetings
    a. Saying "Hello"
    b. Shaking hands
    c. Importance of making eye contact

2. Answering the telephone

3. Asking permission to leave the room

4. Saying "Thank You"

5. Proper behavior in a restaurant

PRESENTATION

1. Carefully open door and enter restaurant

2. Do not make loud noises in the restaurant

3. Wait patiently for hostess to recognize you

4. Sit quietly until your name is called

5. When you hear your name, follow the hostess to your booth

6. Slide carefully into your booth

7. Do not play with the silverware

8. Keep your hands at your side or in your lap

9. Do not interrupt when others are ordering food
10. Place napkin in lap
11. Ask politely for others to pass salt, catsup and other items
12. When you are finished with your meal, thank your waitress for the meal
13. Leave your booth quietly, so as not to disturb others
14. Open the door gently and be courteous to those entering and exiting the restaurant

Your child is probably eager to learn the skills needed to dress himself. Thus, practicing skills in this last category, Care of Oneself, will help him achieve this independence.

D. CARE OF ONESELF

1. Dressing and Undressing Oneself

2. Caring for clothes

3. Polishing shoes

4. Lacing shoes

5. Tying shoelaces

6. Learning how to zip

7. Learning how to put on and take off

a. shoes

b. mittens

When you give each presentation to your child make sure that you use clear actions. Try to use as few words as possible. It is imperative that you focus your child's attention on checking for perfection. This way, your child can see for himself whether or not he has completed the task satisfactorily, and he will not fear disapproval from you if he has made some errors.

Montessori knew that when a child sees a task that he wishes to understand, his will is attracted to it. One can actually see the satisfaction written upon the child's face. The child enthusiastically repeats the action over and over again, each time learning something new about himself and his environment. He is never satisfied by watching others do tasks that he wishes to do himself. A child learns by actively participating in The Practical Life Skills. He needs to be involved in the task in order to fully appreciate it.

Some of the skills involved in learning to take care of oneself can be practiced by using an I Can Dress Myself Board. Some toy stores

I CAN DRESS MYSELF BOARD

may have a similar version in stock. However, if you have the time and want to save a lot of money you can make one yourself. To make an I Can Dress Myself Board like the one pictured on page 28, you will need to purchase heavy posterboard measuring 22" x 28." If possible, purchase a lively yellow or orange colored posterboard. You will use this board to mount the following learning aids.

To teach your child lacing you will need to purchase a pair of old tennis shoes from a thrift store; or, if possible, use an older pair of your own. First, cut the lacing section from the rest of the shoe. Then, repeat this procedure with the other shoe. Next, mount both lacing sections onto the posterboard using either a sturdy tape or non-toxic glue.

To give your child practice working with a zipper you can use an old jacket or shirt. Once again look at the picture of the I Can Dress Myself Board. Notice how the jacket pieces have been evenly separated and mounted onto the poster-board. It is important that you line the pieces up perfectly so that your child can zip up the jacket pieces without difficulty.

You can also give your child practice working with snaps and hooks & eyes by including the following materials on the I Can Dress Myself Board. You will need to sew snaps and hooks & eyes onto pieces of old cloth and then mount the finished pieces onto the poster-board. Once again, be sure that you line the pieces up perfectly so that your child can easily fasten the hooks & eyes and snaps.

Keep in mind that when you present these skills to your child you must include a step by step instruction of how to compete each task.

Finally, you will want your child to have ample practice learning how to button. You probably have an old shirt or blouse that you can use. However, the buttons and button holes may be too small. If this is the case you should remove these smaller buttons and sew on larger buttons in their place. You will undoubtedly have to make the button holes larger; however, by using the larger buttons and button holes your child will not become frustrated while learning this task. Keep in mind that your child is just developing his hand dexterity. Therefore, remember to buy snap fasteners, hooks & eyes, buttons and other learning materials for the I Can Dress Myself Board in the largest size possible.

THREE PERIOD LESSON

Dr. Montessori often made use of the Three Period Lesson when teaching new terminology to children. The Three Period Lesson consists of "presenting" a child with a new concept, asking your child to "show you" that he understands what has been presented and finally, determining if he can correctly "identify" and "pronounce" the name of the new concept that you have presented to him.

You can use the Three Period Lesson to teach your child color identification, number recognition and shape recognition to name a few. Let's use the Three Period Lesson to illustrate how you can help your child learn color identification.

First, obtain four empty wooden spools. Paint two of them red and the other two blue. (You may also use two spools of red thread and two spools of blue thread.) If you don't sew, then use two pieces of red cloth and two pieces of blue cloth. For this illustration, however, I will use the blue and red colored spools.

Period One - Pick up one of the red spools and tell your child that this represents the color "red." Put the red spool down. Next, pick up one of the blue spools and tell your child that this is the color "blue." When you say "red" or "blue" raise your voice slightly and emphasize these words a bit. Repeat Period One again before proceeding on to Period Two.

Period Two - Place a blue spool and red spool in front of your child. Ask your child to show you the red one. Then ask him to show you the blue one. Next, mix the red and blue spools. Once again ask your child to show you which spool is red and which is blue. You can actually make a game out of this. Hide the blue and red spools nearby. Then, ask your child to show you where the blue ones are. If he has correctly shown you where the blue ones were hidden then ask him to show you where the red ones are hidden.

If your child has a nebulous concept of which ones are blue and which are red, then you will need to review Period One again.

However, if your child has a clear understanding of what each color represents then you may proceed on to Period Three.

Period Three - You will now want to determine if your child can clearly identify and correctly pronounce blue and red. Place the blue spool in front of him and ask him to tell you the color. Your child should respond by clearly saying the name. Repeat this exercise using the red spool.

As you can see, the Three Period Lesson can be used to help your child learn many concepts. Fox example, to help your child learn the names of animals you can present various pictures of animals to your child. First, present two pictures of two different animals and then proceed as when you helped your child learn the colors blue and red.

The Three Period Lesson can also be used to help your child learn opposites. Your child can learn words associated with comparisons like big vs. small by first presenting him with a small book. During the second period you will want the child to demonstrate that he can accurately show you a large book and then a small book. Finally, during the third period you will want the child to correctly identify whether you have a big or small book in your hand.

The Three Period Lesson can also be used to help your child learn the names of musical instruments, fish and plants, to mention a few. However, it is important to remember that the Three Period Lesson should always be presented to your child in a relaxed setting. You should speak in a calm, confident manner to your child. Montessori felt that children learn best when they are allowed to absorb knowledge at their own rate. Therefore, you as a parent must be patient. Introduce the Three Period Lesson to your child when you feel relaxed. Obviously, if you feel rushed your child will sense this and he may not be able to concentrate fully. Thus, your time together will not be as productive and enjoyable as it could be.

PRESENTING GEOMETRICAL SHAPES TO YOUR CHILD

As you have discovered, your three year old has many questions about his environment. He is eager to learn the names of the objects that surround him. He enjoys classifying these objects according to color, size and shape.

You can help your child learn how to classify geometrical forms like circles, triangles and rectangles by either purchasing plastic geometrical forms at your nearby toy store or by making these geometrical forms yourself. First, buy several sheets of lightweight posterboard. If possible, purchase the posterboard in as many primary colors as you can.

Use the posterboard to cut out circles, equilateral triangles, scalene triangles, right angle triangles, pentagons, hexagons, octagons, ovals, trapezoids, rectangles and other geometrical forms that you wish to present.

Use the Three Period Lesson to introduce the geometrical forms and to review color identification. The initial Three Period Lesson should be spent presenting a geometrical form such as a right angled triangle. After you have determined that your child can clearly identify and pronounce right angled triangle, then you can use the Three Period Lesson to introduce colored right angled triangles.

To help your child learn the difference between a red right angled triangle and a blue right angled triangle you will need to use two sheets of blue and red posterboard. Cut out both blue right angled triangles and red right angled triangles. Then use the Three Period Lesson to reinforce color identification.

Encourage your child to trace the right angled triangles. Then, supply him with large sized crayons and have him color in the right angled triangles using primary colors.

You will undoubtedly want to repeat this entire process with other geometric forms. However, once your child can accurately pronounce and identify circles, triangles and rectangles, you will want to supply him with plenty of paper and crayons and watch him creatively use the posterboard geometrical forms. He will find that by overlapping the forms he can trace and color interesting patterns. He may begin to see these patterns on clothing, tile floors and paintings, to name a few. Besides developing an appreciation for art, these exercises help your child prepare for writing and geometry.

Your three year old will be anxious to repeat all of the exercises that have been discussed. You will see him strive for perfection if he is allowed the freedom to absorb the concepts at his own pace. The Practical Life Exercises obviously require much practice. Each task attempted by your child should be completed. He should be discouraged from starting and quitting multiple tasks during one of your learning sessions together. He will fail to achieve confidence in his ability if he continually quits before successfully completing a task.

Your role during these learning sessions should be that of a presenter and observer. Once you present the exercise to your child you must step back and let him try to imitate your actions. Stifle your tendencies to become actively involved. It may be frustrating at times to watch your child make errors.

However, your child actually learns from these errors.

If he has a lot of difficulty completing the exercises then you will want to repeat your presentation of the exercises. Encourage your child to pay close attention to what you are doing. Then give him ample time to try again.

Encourage your child to practice these exercises even after he reaches his fourth birthday. Some exercises, like the Practical Life Exercises, should be gradually incorporated into his everyday life. He will want to assume certain responsibilities like hanging up his clothes, throwing out the trash and feeding his pet, to name a few. Of course you will be pleased to see your toddler developing a good self concept and a sense of responsibility.

CHAPTER IV
Your Four Year Old's
Need For Adventure

Your four year old has become more sophisticated in the manner in which he interacts with others and in the way he views his world. Yet, paradoxically, he is still very inquisitive about the world around him.

Your four year old loves to have you read to him. He is fascinated with what the written word has to offer. As you read, he learns more about the world. Undoubtedly, he will ask you many questions and thus learn much during these special times that are shared. Besides helping your child increase his vocabulary level, you will be helping him learn much about reading.

He will learn that stories have a beginning, middle and ending. By asking your child questions about the story you will be exposing him to reading comprehension.

    It is important that you provide your child with a varied appetite for reading. Besides storybooks you might consider including factual books that have colorful pictures of animals, airplanes, fish, reptiles and the like.

    Your four year old will love looking through these factual books. He will have many questions about what he sees. Thus, you will give your child the opportunity to see how "reading" can provide a wealth of information. By watching you read the answers to his questions, he sees what a useful tool reading can be.

If you are in the process of planning to take a family vacation it is often useful to obtain factual books about places that you plan to visit. You will also want to do a little extra research about the history and geography of the region you will be visiting.

Children are very curious about their new surroundings and are delighted when you can answer their questions. Don't assume that your child understands everything. He may feel excited or even overwhelmed if the travel schedule is hectic and the family is visiting many places in a relatively short span of time. Take time during breakfast, lunch and dinner to discuss what the family has seen. This family time is comforting to the young child and he will especially enjoy participating in conversations in a relaxed environment.

We often think that a child has to be at least six or seven to benefit from vacations or short outings. However, this is not the case. Many four year olds are delighted to visit new places and meet new people.

If you don't have the time or you don't want to spend the money right now you might consider taking your four year old on short outings. If, for example, you live near the beach, your child has the opportunity to learn much about sea life. First, visit your local library and learn as much as you can about sea life. Acquaint or reacquaint yourself with

the sea life terminology so that you will be knowledgeable about sea shells, sea gulls and other sea
related life. Next year when your child is five, you
can discuss ecological concerns like oil spills, the
water cycle, food chains and so forth. However,
keep in mind that you are not expected to be an
expert in oceanography. Your role is simply to
present a different environment to your child and
allow him to absorb what he needs from this
experience.

If you are fortunate enough to live near a
farm and are knowledgeable about farm life, then
by all means make arrangements for your child to
visit one. Your child will love to see the farm
animals in their natural habitat. Undoubtedly, he
will be full of questions, so if possible, arrange for
you and your child to talk to the people who live
and work on the farm. This will be one exciting
experience that your child will talk about for years
to come.

Wherever you live, you'll find plenty of
places nearby to visit together. Each region
is unique in its flora and fauna and as you
will discover, outings are not only educa-

tional for your four year old but can also be fun for your entire family.

OBSERVATION OF THE WORLD AROUND HIM

Montessori knew that children learn much from observation exercises. Thus, she devised materials and exercises to help the child discover, make comparisons and see like relationships in his environment.

This next discussion will cover many exercises that your child can practice at home. Obviously, there are other exercises which are available in Montessori schools. Moreover, there are also numerous toy companies specializing in Montessori materials, most of which would be more than happy to provide you with mail catalogs or brochures. However, you can implement all of the suggestions thus far discussed in this book, and by doing so, save a lot of money.

Besides including basic Montessori philosophy, I have incorporated many of my own ideas into this book. Many of the suggestions thus mentioned have been used by me while tutoring children on a one to one basis or while in a classroom setting. My ideas reflect a basic

Montessori philosophy coupled with today's technology.

As you study these sensorial exercises, keep in mind that you may have museums, historical sites, observatories and the like close to home which could provide other excellent exercises in observation. Children love creativity and will appreciate these varied educational observational exercises.

We learn a lot about the environment by using smell, sight and taste. Therefore, to help your child develop a heightened awareness of the differences in taste and sight you will want to present this next set of exercises. First, obtain four pairs of small plastic bottles. The bottles should be uniform in size and color. If possible, obtain bottles which are capped and have droppers. Since this exercise will help your child differentiate among sweet, sour, bitter and salty, you will want your child to pay close attention to your presentation.

First, get a plastic cup and fill it with water. Then, fill each pair of bottles with a different flavor, i.e., two with a sour solution, two with a sweet solution, two with a bitter solution and two with a salty solution. (Make sure that the ingredients you use are non-toxic. If your child is a diabetic or subject to allergies, you may want to check with your child's pediatrician first.) Next, pick up one of the bottles from the first pair, remove the cap, and place a drop of the solution on your finger. After you have tasted it you will announce that it is "sweet." Now, drink some water from the plastic cup to rinse your mouth. Next, encourage your child to test the sweet solution as you did. If your child does this successfully you may proceed with the other flavors. After your child has successfully identified each of the flavors, encourage him to match the flavors using the pairs of bottles.

After your child has repeated this exercise several times, he should be quite knowledgeable about identifying which foods are bitter, which are sweet and so forth. He will more fully appreciate how different food tastes and hopefully he will expand his diet to include food items that are new to him.

OLFACTORY EXERCISES

For this next exercise you can use your own discretion as to how much you want to spend. You probably have a store close by which sells fragrance potpourri packets. These packets can usually be purchased separately according to scent. Many stores have a wide array of fragrances to select from, i.e., rose, mint, lavender and so on. Select four fragrances and purchase four pairs, i.e., two for each fragrance.

When presenting this exercises, you will want to select one fragrance at a time. Let's say to simplify things that you have chosen to present the fragrance "rose." Pick up the packet, smell it, and say it is "rose". Next, invite your child to do the same. After your child has correctly identified the four scents encourage him to correctly match the potpourri packets according to scent.

Later, you may want to purchase additional different scented potpourri packets so that your child can experience as many delightful scents as possible. Your child will be enthusiastic about completing this exercise if you relate it to relevant things like identifying the aroma of a freshly baked apple pie or the wonderful fragrance of the rose garden nearby.

Your child also learns much about his environment through touch. One exercise which is both educational and challenging for him involves identifying geometrical objects by touch alone. Montessori originally used solid geometrical objects. These solid forms may be obtained by contacting Lakeshore, ABC or by contacting some of the other educational toy companies listed in the appendix of this book. I have successfully used the geometrical forms made from posterboard for this exercise, and I feel that you can easily make the forms as well.

First, draw triangles, rectangles, ovals, circles and any other geometrical forms that you wish to present on a sheet of light to medium weight posterboard. Then, cut out at least two of every geometrical form that you intend to use. To make this exercise even more challenging for your child, make the forms in different sizes. Next, spread the forms out in front of you and invite your child to watch the presentation.

First, close your eyes and randomly select one of the forms in front of you. Pick up the form and lightly trace around its outline with your index finger. With your eyes still closed, announce the proper geometrical name for the form that you are now holding. Repeat this exercise. Then invite your child to try it.

It sometimes seems that children love to touch everything in their environment, and many times we have to tell them that they must keep their hands to themselves. Therefore, your child should really enjoy completing this exercise. You will probably find that your child will want to repeat this exercise many times and you should encourage him to do so.

GETTING READY TO WRITE

In order for a child to write he must be able to successfully orient himself in time and space. He must also be cognizant of direction and laterality. By tracing and manipulating geometric shapes he learns how to hold a pencil. The Practical Life Exercises provide the child with lightness of touch. For example, the child develops eye/hand coordination and dominant hand preference by exercises like polishing and dusting. He learns the four basic writing symbols, the vertical l, the horizontal –, the diagonal /, and the circle O, by tracing the geometrical forms.

At this time, additional exercises which give needed practice in preparation for writing should be introduced to your child.

One preparatory exercise, Walking the Line, is introduced to children as young as three years of age. This is a must for the four year old preparing to read and write.

At many Montessori schools a line is made with either chalk or paint. (You can easily make such a line with chalk). Be sure to draw a line that is at least 20 feet in length. Then practice walking on the line, heel to

toe, heel to toe. Next, invite your child to follow you. Repeat this exercise several times. Once you feel that your child is comfortable walking on the line, have him practice this exercise in time to music. Preferably you should use a march, and to make it even more challenging, let your child walk in time to the music while playing a toy tambourine. This exercise will be beneficial in helping the child to orient himself in time and space. Other exercises are also useful at this time. Exercises that involve balancing, like hopping and skipping, are also useful in helping the young child prepare for reading and writing. Moreover, many young children love to play games like hopscotch.

Another exercise which will be beneficial in helping to prepare your child for both reading and writing involves working with Sandpaper Letters. Montessori devised this exercise to help the child visualize the letters through touch.

You can easily make these letters by purchasing the appropriate supplies from specialty stores in your neighborhood. First, you will need to purchase several sheets of lightweight posterboard. Next, purchase some non-toxic glue. Finally, purchase some sandpaper and you are all set to make the Sandpaper Letters exercise!

If you do not live near a city you may have a little difficulty finding everything you need. However, you can probably purchase the sandpaper from your local paint or lumber store. Many small neighborhood stationery or art supply shops carry posterboard in different weights and sizes. Look in your telephone directory for the stores closest to you.

The Sandpaper Letters should be at least 2-1/2" in height. Obviously, if you intend to make the letters 3" high you will need to purchase more sandpaper and lightweight posterboard.

Use the posterboard to draw and cut out letters A to Z. Next, place each individual letter against the smooth side of the sandpaper. Trace around the letters onto the smooth side of the sandpaper so that you have an exact outline of every letter in the alphabet. Next, cut out the sandpaper letter outlines and glue the smooth side of the sandpaper letters onto the poster-board letters. You should now have 26 letters for the Sandpaper Letters exercise.

The Sandpaper Letters exercise is your child's first introduction to the alphabet. Therefore, it is important that you don't hurry through the letters. In fact, it is important that you only present three letters at a time. I feel that it is better to present the consonants first and the vowels last.

Choose three letters that are very different in form, i.e., "s," "n," and "p." (You wouldn't want to select "b," "d" or "p," "q" because to your young child these letters look very much alike and such a presentation would be quite confusing.)

Next, place letters "n", "s", and "p" on the table near your child. Trace the letter "n" with your first (index) and second fingers of your hand. Concurrently, make the "n" sound. Then, encourage your child to trace the letter "n." At this time the two of you might discuss words beginning with "n" like night, nine and nickel.

Next, present the letter "s" in the same manner in which you presented the letter "n." To ascertain whether or not your child can accurately differentiate the letter "n" from the letter "s," ask your child to point to the letter "n." Ask him if he knows the sound for the letter "n." Then ask him to show you the letter "s." He should also be able to tell you what "s" sounds like. If he seems confused you will want to review the presentation again.

If you feel that your child has a sound concept of the letters "n" and "s," then you can introduce the third letter.

After you are absolutely certain that your child can easily identify these three letters, select three more letters and use the same presentation to help your child learn these additional letters. Continue in this manner until you have covered all of the letters of the alphabet. When you cover the vowels a, e, i, o and u it is best to present the short vowel sound first. For example, when introducing the letter "a," say words beginning with the short "a" vowel like apple and acrobat. Next, when you introduce the "e" sound, say words beginning with the short "e" sound like egg and elephant. When introducing the short "i" vowel sound, you will want to include words like Indian and igloo. Words beginning with the short "o" vowel sound like octopus and olive help the child recognize this sound in words like box and fox. Finally, you will want to include words like umbrella, up and under when introducing the short "u" vowel sound. Your child will love tracing his fingers over the letters and saying the associated sounds.

At this time you can also help your child's vocabulary grow by having him match up two identical pictures while the two of you discuss the correct name of the object in the pictures and the object's beginning sound. To do this exercise properly you will need to draw a set for each object you select. In each set you will have two pictures that are identical in every way. If you decide to draw two cats, make sure that they are exactly alike. If you can't draw, then purchase sets of picture postcards or purchase sets from Shapes, Etc. Remember to buy two of each object.

You can also use photo stickers, identical snapshots, stamps and so forth. Be sure that you don't bombard your child with too many sets at one time.

Initially start with three or four sets, and once you feel that your child can easily match up the pictures, introduce additional sets. Later, to add a challenging dimension to this exercise, provide labels for the pictures.

Using small index cards, neatly print the name of object in large bold letters. Remember to make two labels for each set. Initially, you will want to present three or four sets at a time.

Place the index card label underneath the appropriate picture. (See page 58.) Then, read the name listed on the index card label. Next, ask your child to find the mate to this picture. Then ask him to place the index card label underneath this picture. Finally, ask your child to name the picture. After you have completed this exercise with three sets, remove the labels and place them to the right of your child. Now ask your child to put the correct labels underneath the corresponding pictures.

You can further help your child prepare for writing and reading when you go to the grocery store. When your child accompanies you to the grocery store and appears interested in identifying the different foods that he sees, you should stop and discuss some of the names of the foods with him. Your child may pick up a can of peaches, recognize it and attempt to read p e a c h e s. He may remember the sound for "p" and thus be very enthused about his discovery. You, in turn, need to show your excitement at his discovery.

If your child seems disinterested in your trip to the grocery store then you may need to

MATCHING LABEL TO PICTURE EXERCISE

try another approach. First, go through old magazines and clip out colorful advertisements for orange juice, peaches and grape juice, to name a few.

During your next trip to the store, purchase some of the foods advertised. Then challenge your child to match the advertisements to the corresponding items that you purchased.

RECOGNITION OF NUMBERS

Soon your child will also need to recognize numbers; thus, Montessori devised what has come to be known as the Sandpaper Numbers exercise. Undoubtedly you will want to make a set of these numbers for your child. Construct the numbers in the way that you constructed the 26 letters for the Sandpaper Letter exercise.

When presenting the Sandpaper Number exercise, present two numbers at a time. Start with numbers 0 and 1. Use the Three Period Lesson to present this exercise. Period One - Trace 0 and 1 with your fingers. When you trace "0" say "0." When you trace "1" say "1." Period Two - Ask your child to show you which number is "0" and which is "1." Then ask him to trace with his fingers "0" and then

"1." Period Three - Pick up the "0" number and ask your child its name. Do the same with "1." Do not rush through this exercise. If necessary, repeat any periods that seemed confusing to your child. Later, introduce the remaining numbers, two at a time, using the Three Period Lesson each time.

By now your child is probably anxious to write. Give him ample paper, a pencil and encourage him to write the four basic writing symbols, i.e., the vertical l, the horizontal –, the diagonal /, and the circle O. Encourage him to always write these symbols as neatly as possible. As you can see, these symbols are used to make the 26 letters of the alphabet, and the numbers 0 to 9.

For example, the letter X is formed by using the diagonal symbol. The lower case letter q is made with a circle symbol and a vertical symbol. The letter Z is formed by using both the horizontal and diagonal symbols. Thus, it is obvious that your child will need to spend much time writing these symbols in preparation for printing the 26 letters of the alphabet.

INDIVIDUALIZING THE EXERCISES

At this stage in your child's development, it is important to be somewhat flexible about what is covered during your learning sessions. You may plan to spend part of the session reviewing the Sandpaper Letters exercise and the rest of the session covering the four basic writing symbols. However, if your child seems absorbed in his work with the Sandpaper Letters exercise then it may be best to let him complete his work.

These exercises allow your child to make discoveries and comparisons around him. Hence, he needs time to make these discoveries and see the differences and similarities in his environment. For example, he may want to spend an entire learning session writing the four basic symbols.

Eventually, he will discover that these symbols form both the 26 letters of the alphabet and numbers. Then he will be ready for a new adventure, the printing of letters.

CHAPTER V

Kindergarten At Home For
Four and Five Year Old Children

Montessori felt that each child learns at his own pace. She felt that given the appropriate materials in a relaxed prepared setting, the child can absorb knowledge that will be useful for his development.

Your child, thus far, has been given the opportunity to develop skills that will help him prepare for reading, writing and math. Many children entering kindergarten haven't had this opportunity. Some of the children in a typical kindergarten setting are four and a half years of age, some are five and the rest are close to six years of age. Yet, the students are treated as though they are all at the same point in their development. Unfortunately, they are expected to progress in a uniform manner and this is often stressful for the child.

By exposing your child to the exercises in this book you will have helped him achieve the confidence that he needs to learn. Some children will become more confident than others, but you, as a parent, play a vital role by providing a "prepared environment" during your learning sessions together. In such an environment your child feels relaxed and eager to learn.

Keep in mind that the exercises described in this book will be useful for the child entering a public or private school. Therefore, encourage your child to do as many of these exercises as possible.

Do not skip any of the preparatory exercises. The preparatory exercises were designed to help your child achieve skills necessary to learn reading and writing, understand math concepts, appreciate his enviroment and become confident in his ability to care for himself.

If your child has successfully completed the preparatory exercises then he is almost ready to begin writing. However, there is one exercise which will further prepare him for writing.

This exercise is often called the Movable Alphabet exercise. You can construct the letters out of posterboard. At this time you may want to review the section on how to construct letters for the Sandpaper Letter exercise, since the procedure is very similar. The only exception is that the posterboard letters will not be covered with sandpaper.

To properly present this exercise you will need the 26 letters constructed out of posterboard, the matching pictures used in a previous exercise and the corresponding labels that your child used to identify the objects in the pictures.

Initially, you and your child will want to review the 26 letters and their sounds. Once you have done this, place the 26 letters in a pile. Then proceed to match up the pictures. It is best to present three sets at a time. Let's say that your three sets include two identical pictures of a cat, two identical pictures of a dog and two identical pictures of a fish. From the pile of 26 letters remove c, a, t, d, o, g, f, i, s and h. Place these letters in a separate pile. Now, encourage your child to place the label entitled cat under

MOVABLE ALPHABET EXERCISE

one of the appropriate pictures. Then, invite him to remove the appropriate letters from the small pile of ten letters. He will then select the letters c, a, t and place them underneath the duplicate picture of the cat. Your child will continue until he has completed these three sets. He will probably want to complete additional sets and you should encourage him to do so. He may eventually want to use the movable alphabet to form words on his own and this too, should be encouraged.

Once again, we see that movement plays an integral part in learning. In this case, we see that movement allows your child to visualize the written letters and words by tracing over the letters. The Sandpaper Letters exercise and Movable Alphabet exercise go hand in hand. While your child touches a letter and repeats its associated sound he is visualizing the image of the letter, which in itself is a preparatory exercise for reading. He feels the letter with his finger and then traces its outline in the same direction in which he will eventually write it. Besides actualizing the movement corresponding to writing he also demonstrates that he is learning how to sight read vowels and consonants.

PRESENTATION OF WRITING AND READ-ING

You can tell when your child is ready to write by first analyzing how well he writes the four basic writing symbols. Your child has been working with the geometrical posterboard shapes for some time now. In fact, he has probably made intricate geometrical designs like the two pictured on page 69. Before the explosion of writing occurs you will observe the following. First you will notice that the vertical lines that your child makes to fill and color the geometrical designs have become singularly even and regular. Next, you will notice that your child has become thoroughly acquainted with the alphabet. In fact, your child probably can recognize the letters by sense of touch alone.. Next, you will observe that your child has composed many words with the movable alphabet.

He is now ready for your presentation on printing of the upper and lower case letters of the alphabet. Introduce two at a time, starting with Aa and proceeding in alphabetical order.

Because your child is so familiar with the alphabet and is proficient with the four basic symbols he may want to print letters and words on his own. You must allow him to do this. Printing on his own and perfecting his penmanship by starting with Aa and of course ending with Zz can go hand in hand.

Soon your child will enjoy incorporating the Movable Alphabet exercise into his printing of new words. Your child might enjoy rhyming games like can, fan, man, ran, by changing the initial consonant. First he uses the movable letters to form these words. Then, he can practice writing these words. Blends can also be reinforced by using the movable letters. Initially, you will want to present short vowel blends like ba-bag, be-beg, bi-big, bo-bog and bu-bug. Later, using index cards you can make blends like ma, me, mi, mo, mu and print words beginning with these blends on separate cards. See page 70. For example, your child would place the cards with blends like "mat," "mall," "mad," "man," "map," under the card with the "ma" blend heading.

GEOMETRICAL EXERCISES

ba	be	bi	bo	bu
bat	Ben	big	Bob	bud
ban	bell	bit	box	bug
ma	me	mi	mo	mu
mad	men	mill	mop	mum
mat	met	mitt	mom	mud
pa	pe	pi	po	pu
Pat	pet	pit	pot	pup
pan	pen	pig	pop	pup

SHORT VOWEL BLENDS EXERCISE

Other games that your child might enjoy include spelling names of pets, like dog, cat and bird, spelling names of motor vehicles like car, bus, cab and train, or spelling names of animals in the zoo.

Most primers and beginning reading books at the first grade level introduce both short and long vowel monosyllable words. Therefore, I feel that it is best to initially introduce the short vowel words only.

Use the movable letters to show your child how he can form short "a" vowel words. First, locate the letter "b." Ask your child to tell you what the letter "b" sounds like. Next, review the short "a" sound. Ask him to say "b" and "a" together. He would say "ba." Now select an ending consonant to make a short vowel word. Show your child that if you put the letters "ba" with the letter "t" you have formed the word "bat." Have your child sound out the letters "b" "a" "t." Now, have him select another ending consonant. He should continue until he has formed several words with the "ba" blend like "bad," "bag" and "ban."

The next blend "be" is occasionally confusing to the young child. Some children have difficulty differentiating between the "be" and "bi" blends. Stress the short "e" in words like "egg," "elephant," "nest," "best" and "rest." Have your child sound out the "be" blend and then encourage him to form words using final consonants like "d" to make a new word, "b" "e" "d."

Now proceed with the "bi" blend. Review what the letter "b" sounds like. Then, review the short "i" vowel sound. Your child should remember that words like "igloo" and "Indian" begin with the short "i" vowel sound. Next, have your child sound out the "bi" blend. Once he has successfully done this, encourage him to locate final consonants like "t" to make the word "bit," "g" to make "big" and so on. Once you have exhausted final consonants for the "bi" blend move on to "bo" and "bu" blends.

To help reinforce what your child has just learned you may want to purchase a spelling link set. These sets come in many forms. Some of the sets allow for spelling of both short and long vowel words. The sets contain multiple cubes which snap together. Each cube has a letter of the alphabet on it. By snapping the cubes together your child can form over 100 words.

Another version of the spelling link consists of three or more cubes which are permanently attached together. Each cube has four letters on it. By twisting the individual cubes the child forms both long and short vowel words. As you will see, these tools often provide hours of fascination for the young child so you may want to consider purchasing one.

Your child will want to know why some words have the short a, e, i, o or u sound while others have the long vowel sound. You will want to explain that when a word contains only one vowel we usually say the word with its short vowel sound. When a monosyllable word contains two vowels we say the first vowel in the word with its long sound while the second vowel remains silent. For example, we pronounce meat with its long "e" vowel sound. The vowel "a" is silent. We do not say "me" "at."

You will also want to introduce decoding of words, and one interesting way in which to do so involves first purchasing a packet of small index cards in a vast array of colors. Each color represents a different category of decoding. You will want to present silent letters like "g" in "gnat"; "k" in "knock" or "knot"; "w" in "wrong" and "write"; phonograms like "wh," "ch," "sh," "ph," "th," "ea," "ir," "or," "qu," "le," "ing" and "tion" and medial sounds like "oi," "oy," "ir" and "er."

Select one color for all words containing the "ch" phonogram. Write words like church, check, chill and chime on index cards of the same color. Next, choose a different color to introduce the "wh" phonogram. Continue in this manner until you have several piles. Your child will appreciate learning to decode these words because they have been printed on these colorful cards. Naturally, you will want to present a few cards at a time, and use the Three Period Lesson to make sure that your child is decoding and pronouncing the words correctly.

Spelling, grammar, oral reading and reading comprehension are interrelated and Montessori felt that they could be presented concurrently. One can certainly see that by presenting each as a separate entity the young child fails to see the relationship of oral reading to spelling and reading comprehension to grammar. If you give your child an inter-disciplinary presentation to language he will gain the reasoning necessary to decode and decipher its meaning.

SPELLING AND ALPHABETIZING EXERCISES

By this time your child probably enjoys working alone and checking his work himself. Thus, you must respect this need and provide him with the appropriate tools in which to do so. He is excited about reciting the alphabet to you and enjoys putting the letters in alphabetical order. However, he needs to check his work from time to time against a control card. On such a card you will have written the letters of the alphabet, as neatly as possible, in alphabetical order.

After your child has demonstrated to you that he has mastered beginning letters, you will want to make up additional control cards. For example, the second set of cards will give your child practice alphabetizing words using the second letter method. On the second control card you will have written words like "aid," "ant" and "apple." The child will look at three index cards and see the words "aid," "ant" and "apple." (On each card he will find a different word beginning with the letter "a.") He will then attempt to place the words in alphabetical order by looking at the second letter. Next, he will check his work against the control card to make certain that he has correctly completed the exercise. Continue to make control cards for the remaining 25 letters of the alphabet and allow him ample time to practice this exercise.

Once your child has demonstrated that he can easily alphabetize words like "be," "bottle" and "bud," you can proceed to present a more difficult alphabetizing exercise using the third letter method. You will want to present him with words like "bee," "begin" and "benefit." Of course, you will need to make up a third set of control cards so that he can continue to check his work.

Alphabetizing words plus spelling rhyming words like "fill," "will," "mill" and "dill" are excellent exercises in spelling. Missing letter exercises like the one pictured on page 77 are also useful for strengthening your

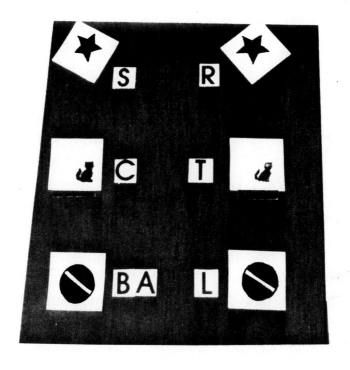

MISSING LETTER EXERCISE

child's spelling ability plus reinforcing his vocabulary knowledge.

GRAMMAR AND READING COMPREHEN-SION

You can reinforce reading comprehension
and introduce grammar by asking your child
probing questions about what he has read. To do
this exercise properly you need to purchase sentence strips at an educational supply company.
Or, you can make some yourself from lightweight
posterboard. Also, keep in mind that you will
need to purchase index cards for this exercise.

For our first example, let's analyze the following sentence. The cat is fat. Print this
sentence as neatly as possible on a sentence strip.
(See page 80.) First, ask your child to read this
sentence to you. Then ask your child to tell "who"
is fat. As you will recall, the subject of the
sentence reveals "who" or "what" the sentence is
about. By responding to your question your child
learns that "cat" is the subject of the sentence.

Do not be too critical if your child informs
you that "the cat" is the subject of the sentence.
As   you   know,   "the"   is   an   article,

but it is often easier for the child to link the article with the subject when responding to your question.

Now, take three index cards and on each card write a different subject which can be used to replace "cat" in this subject. Once again look at the picture on page 80. If I place the index card with the word "pig" printed on it over the word "cat," I have changed the meaning of the sentence. My sentence now reads as follows: The pig is fat. Ask your child to read this new sentence. When you ask him to tell you who is fat, he should now respond by telling you that "the pig" is fat. If he seems confused, you will want to review this part of the grammar exercise again.

To introduce the idea of descriptive words and adjectives, you will ask your child to tell you what kind of cat is mentioned in this sentence, i.e., small, fat or thin, to name a few. To reinforce this concept, introduce a second sentence strip that includes more than one adjective. Study the next sentence for a moment. The cat is tan and white. Your child is now introduced to a sentence that contains

BEGINNING GRAMMAR EXERCISE

more than one descriptive word. He sees that both words "tan" and "white" are needed to accurately describe the cat.

As you can readily see, your child learns much about grammar during these question and answer periods. However, he is also increasing his reading comprehension. He is actually analyzing the meaning of a word and its relationship to the other words in a sentence.

COMMAND CARDS

Command Cards, like the ones pictured on page 82, help your child in the areas of reading and grammar. A command is neatly printed on an index card. Your child reads what is written and then acts out the command. This is a fun exercise for him to do. Moreover, in the future when he reads a command like "Look at the picture!" he will learn that the verb is "look" and that (you), the subject is understood.

CLASSIFIED READING CARDS

By now your child has been exposed to numerous reading exercises which have prepared him for the Classified Reading Cards exercise. Look at the pictures of trees on page 84. Notice how a different part of the tree is shaded in

COMMAND CARDS

each picture. In one picture the truck is shaded. In another picture the leaves are shaded. This is done so that the child's attention is focused on the particular shaded area, and it is easier for him to learn the names associated with the various components of a tree.

Classified Reading Cards provide another excellent opportunity for children to learn details. Often, children read about flowers or birds, yet they know little about the anatomy and physiology of these living things. Thus, Classified Reading Cards help the child focus on the details that make up these living things.

Let's assume that you want to present your child with a lesson on how an apple is made. First, you will need to include at least four identical pictures of a tree. If you want to depict the fruit, in this case an apple, you will want to include five pictures. Number each picture so that you have 1 through 5. Picture 1 illustrates the branches of the tree. Picture 2 illustrates the trunk of the tree. Picture 3 illustrates the roots of the tree. Finally, Picture 4 illustrates the leaves of the tree. Since you will be presenting a fruit bearing

CLASSIFIED READING CARDS

tree you will want to include a fifth picture illustrating the apple. On each picture you will notice that a different part is shaded in red. As discussed before, this helps the child focus on the part of the tree presented at that moment. It is not enough that the child merely memorize the names of the part of the tree, the child must understand the function of each of these parts.

Naturally, the Three Period Lesson is presented, however, once you are certain that your child recognizes the names and positions of the various parts of the tree, you will want to spend time discussing each individual part.

First you will discuss the importance of an apple in our diet. Then, slice an apple in half and show your child the seeds inside the apple. Explain to the child that the apple was once a small seed, and that without these seeds we wouldn't have apples.

Next, explain to your child that a seed cannot become an apple unless it has a special environment in which to develop into its potential. Once planted in water the seed receives nourishment from the soil.

Now, place an index card with the word "roots" written on it and place the card under the picture with the roots area shaded in red. Explain that the seed then grows into a young tree with roots which will insure constant nourishment. These roots are like long spidery fingers that draw up moisture and nutrients from the soil.

This moisture and nourishment is carried up through the "trunk" of the tree. Then, place the card with the word "trunk" written on it under the picture of the trunk shaded in red. Explain that the trunk is also important because it provides shape and support for the branches. At this point you will want to place the card with "branches" written on it under the picture with the branches shaded in red.

Further explain that the moisture that was drawn up from the roots through the trunk now reaches the "branches." Direct your child's attention to the picture of the branches shaded in red. Then, place the card with "branches" written on it underneath this picture.

As you continue with your presentation, you will want to further elaborate that it is on these branches that "leaves" appear. Your child's attention should now be focused on the card with "leaves" written upon it and the picture with the leaves shaded in red. You might explain that flowers also appear on the branches. It is from these flowers that the apples are formed.

Now focus your child's attention on the apple. Explain that the apples remain on the tree until they are ripe. Some apples, like Red Delicious apples are picked when they are deep red in color. Finally, explain to your child that now that the apple tree is bearing fruit the process is complete.

The Classified Reading Cards can also be used to help your child learn more about flowers, birds, butterflies and fish, to name a few. For example, you can make a set of Classified Reading Cards and pictures describing the different parts of a fish. In each picture a different part of the fish would be shaded in red so that the child's attention will be focused on learning the different parts that are united together to form a fish.

Classified Reading Cards also help the child pay close attention to the details in various pictures.

Because the preceding exercises have given the young child the ability to clearly compare, analyze and notice details in pictures, it is often wise to introduce some of the fine arts to him. As you know, the fine arts are often called "The Humanities." The name *humanities* is very apropos since music, art, architecture, literature and drama all deal with and reflect the human condition.

By studying famous works of art, the child sees how intricate hues, lines, dimension and form converge on the canvas to express a part of the artist's inner soul. Moreover, because the paintings reflect a certain era, i.e., Byzantine, Renaissance, Rococo and so forth, the child learns how the painting reflected attitudes displayed during that particular time in our history.

It is often wise to present both the art and music of a given period concurrently. If the child is exposed to music and art of the Renaissance period he not only sees the rebirth or renaissance displayed in painting completed during that time but also hears the embellishments added to musical compositions that were written during this exciting time in our history. Thus, the child sees and hears how new illuminating ideas were being expressed in the humanities. He sees the binary fusion of art and music and how it reflects a particular era in history. Your child needs to be given the opportunity to learn as much as possible about the periods of art like the Byzantine, Renaissance, Rococo, Impressionism and so on. By comparing the different styles of, for example, the Renaissance to that of the Rococo, your child will develop the ability to detect the intricate subtleties that distinguish the two periods in our history.

First, go to a local library and reacquaint yourself with art history. Take notes about particular paintings and sculptures that you want your child to recognize. If possible, write to museums that have these paintings and sculptures and inquire as to whether they sell postcards (reproductions) of the famous artwork.

Some of the museums do have gift shops and/or book stores where these postcards are sold. You may be able to purchase some of these postcards by mail; however, remember to purchase two identical postcards for each type selected.

Once you have obtained the postcards you need, you can further classify these reproductions according to period and/or artist. Use the Three Period Lesson to introduce this exercise. It is best to introduce one period or one artist as a time. Then, at a later time, use the Three Period Lesson to help your child differentiate among periods or artists. By doing these exercises, children gain experience in identifying great works of art. When your child has an opportunity to visit a nearby gallery or museum, he will be able to appreciate the originals more fully.

An introduction to the humanities wouldn't be complete without including literature. Because the young child has learned simple grammar at a relatively young age, he revels in the opportunity to listen to poetry and act out what he has learned. Words have special meaning to him and he learns much about people and their feelings by listening to great works of literature. The fine arts, then, further expose the child to what life is like for people in distant lands. The child learns that each person is unique in appearance, culture and so forth. It is this uniqueness that makes each person special. The child also learns that although each person may be unique, he still may have the same feeling, i.e., the feelings of loneliness, feelings of sadness and feelings of happiness that are universal. Thus, mankind is bound together in a special way.

DRAWING AND OBSERVATION

Your child is learning a lot about the different famous artists and he is being influenced by one or more of the styles exhibited by these painters. He will have made mental notes about the techniques or styles that each artist has used. He will then proceed to incorporate into his own compositions what has influenced him most.

Encourage your child to continue tracing the geometrical forms. You may want to make various geometric exercises, like the ones pictured on pages 93 and 94. Lightweight poster-board is used for both exercises.

The various geometrical forms are outlined using fine, medium and broad point markers. The child is then invited to place solid cardboard geometrical forms over the appropriate geometrical outlines. This exercise can be introduced long before the child reaches four years of age. However, it is important to place special emphasis on it now, when he is studying geometrical forms.

To help your child increase his power of observation and fuse art with science, you can present your child with a butterfly stained glass painting project. You will need to purchase transparent parchment paper on which you will outline a butterfly in black. See page 84 for an illustration of a stained glass project using an outline of a butterfly and an outline of a flower.

Then, visit your local library and borrow a book about butterflies. While reading the book take notes about the different types of butterflies so that you can provide answers to your child's questions. Select the picture

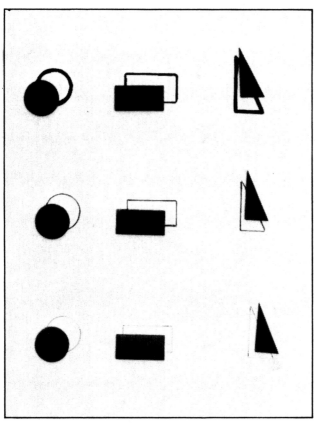

GEOMETRICAL FORMS

OBSERVATION EXERCISES

of the butterfly that you want your child to learn about. Draw an outline of the butterfly that you selected, i.e., Buckeye, Baltimore, Hackberry and so forth, on a sheet of parchment paper. Make sure that you draw an excellent reproduction of the butterfly selected. Once you feel satisfied with your outline, take another sheet of parchment paper and draw another identical outline of the butterfly. This second outline will later be given to your child.

Next, using color crayons, color the butterfly, paying close attention to which colors were used in your library book. Remember, you want your drawing of the selected butterfly to be as authentic as possible.

Once you have completed the coloring, invite your child now to color the s e c - ond outline. Since the parchment paper is transparent, it yields itself very nicely to a stained glass effect. Although your child will periodically love to hold his work up against the window where he sees how the sunlight intensifies the butterfly's colors, encourage the child to study your outline so that he makes mental notes of the different colors. Later, you will want your child to study and color in outlines for other types of butterflies. So, encourage your child to notice details like the body length, antennae length and so on.

Your child should want to check his work to see if he is accurately reproducing your finished work. You should also encourage him to color on both sides of the parchment so the colors look deep and rich.

GEOGRAPHY

In many Montessori schools you will see children as young as four years of age working with Land and Water Form models. The Three Period Lesson can be presented to help your child recognize the following land forms: Island, Peninsula, Cape, Isthmus, Lake, Gulf, Bay and Strait.

You can draw the land forms like those depicted on page 97 and have your child place a corresponding index identifying card under each picture. The pictures on page 97 depict the following:

1a. Island   1b. Lake
2a. Peninsula   2b. Gulf

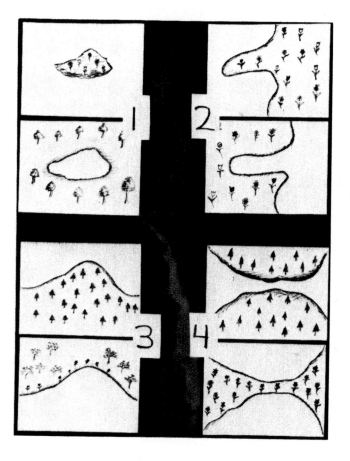

LAND FORMS

3a. Cape
3b. Bay
4a. Strait
4b. Isthmus

It is best to present two land forms at a time to your child. Therefore, the Three Period Lesson is an excellent means to help your child pronounce, identify and compare the different land forms.

It is important that the land forms not be presented in a vacuum. Draw your child's attention to examining these land forms on regional maps, country maps and the world globe. Discuss with your child how each land form is a determining factor in agriculture, fishing, population growth, industry and residential property.

To make world maps more meaningful to your child, you might first consider purchasing a world map from your local general bookstore or college bookstore. Then, purchase used postal stamps, one for each of the countries, and help your child locate on the map where each stamps should be placed. Stamps can usually be purchased at hobby shops or stamp and coin shops. If you want to present stamp collecting to your child, you may want to invest in stamp hinges. However, glueing the stamps onto the map often works best.

Your child may have many questions about the pictures on the stamps, i.e., of queens, kings, causes, flowers, animals, religious symbols, flags, famous battles and so forth. This will give you many excellent opportunities to discuss topics like history, geography, botany and religion with your child. Naturally you won't want your child to glue all of the stamps onto the map during one learning session. This would be a frustrating and exhausting experience for the child. If your child located only seven to ten countries during one learning session he will feel excited about his accomplishment and be open to a short discussion on geography or history.

TELLING TIME

Hopefully, you and your child have discussed other parts of the world and he has discovered that there are differences in climate, culture, government, seasons and, in particular, time. If not, this would be an excellent opportunity to make telling time relevant to your child. Then, proceed on to the presentation.

The actual presentation involves a discussion of the minute hand and the hour hand. First, make matching sets of clocks set to various hours of the 24 hour cycle. Next, present the three sets of time and then encourage your child to match up the sets. He should put the cards showing the identical time side by side.

Once your child has mastered telling time to the hour then introduce telling time to the half hour using the same method. Then, show the time differences around the world. Do not pressure him to memorize or learn the exact time differences, because at this stage in his development he may find it quite frustrating to do so.

MORE MATH EXERCISES

Your three year old has worked with the geometrical forms and the Sandpaper Numbers. Now it is time to introduce additional math exercises. The Spindle Box shown on page 102 helps your child equate a given quantity with a particular number.

Convert an old tie box into a spindle box by dividing it into ten equal sections. Use either small index cards or posterboard to serve as partitions. Be sure to glue the partitions in place so that they don't slip back and forth. Crayons are colorful and make excellent spindles.

Present the exercise by focusing your child's attention on the first five sections of the box. Say "zero" and point to the first section in the Spindle Box. Once you and your child agree that "zero" signifies "nothing," then proceed on to the next section.

Remove one spindle (crayon) and say "one." Place the crayon back into the second section and again say "one." Continue in this manner until you have completed the first five sections of the Spindle Box. Now invite your child to do the exercise. Once you feel your child has mastered 0 - 4, then proceed on to the remaining numbers, 5 - 9.

In addition to completing this exercise you will want to reinforce number recognition by asking your child to bring you three pencils, five pieces of paper, eight envelopes and so forth.

SPINDLE BOX

The Counting Game like the one pictured on page 104 is another exercise that helps the child equate a given quantity with its corresponding number. Moreover, many children love to play this game independently for hours at a time.

For this exercise you will need one lightweight posterboard measuring 22" x 28," ten numeral cards from 1 to 10 and 55 counters. The 55 counters can be made from construction paper and the numeral cards can be made by cutting small index cards in half and neatly printing the numerals on these cards.

Present this exercise to your child by first placing the cards in mixed order. Then, ask your child to find the card that comes first. After he has located "1" tell him to place "1" on the far upper left of the posterboard. Finally, ask your child to place the correct amount of the counters under "1." Proceed in this matter until your child has fully completed the exercise.

EXERCISES IN MEASURING

Montessori frequently noted that children learn best when given hands on opportunity. Thus, it is not enough to simply tell a child

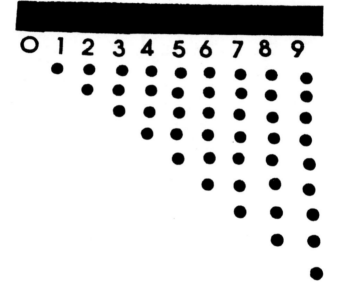

THE COUNTING GAME

that one yard is equal to three feet. To make such an exercise more meaningful to a child it is better to take three rulers and place them end to end and then let the child see for himself that in fact three rulers are equal to one yard.

Next, you will want to encourage your child to measure things in his environment. Give him a ruler and encourage him to measure a crayon or a pen. Then ask him if he would use a ruler or yardstick to measure the following: a front door, a pencil, an eraser, a book and a window. For circular objects, like a wastepaper basket or a globe, your child can simply place a string around these objects, mark off the length, and then place the string next to a yardstick to determine the precise measurement. This exercise allows the child to further make comparisons about objects around him.

TIPS FOR THE BILINGUAL PARENT

If you are bilingual you have an excellent opportunity to expose your child to more than one language. First, you will find that because your child has been at a sensitive period to learn new languages, he has readily absorbed the grammar of this new language.

Some Montessori schools offer instruction in a foreign language and you too may want to incorporate some of these ideas into the learning sessions in your home. First, emphasis is placed on perfecting the child's oral vocabulary in a second language. This can best be accomplished by exposing the child to the native language and culture in an interesting way. Ideally, a native speaking person from a country should present the foreign language to the child. If at all possible, the child should also be exposed to the culture, so that he can experience under what circumstances the language is spoken.

Instead of just memorizing words, the child should be exposed first hand to the meanings of these words. Let's use the Spanish language as an example. A native Spanish speaking individual would present the lessons, conversing most of the time in Spanish. The environment would be a prepared one, complete with Spanish decor, Spanish books and a Spanish calendar. The person presenting would speak in simple commands to the child. She would present the child with the equivalent Spanish words for the parts of the body, i.e., hands and so forth, by presenting the Three Period Lesson. She would also present the names of colors in Spanish by using the Three Period Lesson technique.

When the child's oral vocabulary is quite proficient, the child should then be introduced to the written language in the same manner used to present English. For example, Sandpaper Letters of the Spanish alphabet would be as follows: a, b, c, ch, d, e, f, g, h, i, j, k, l, ll, m, n, ñ, o, p, q, r, rr, s, t, u, v, w, x, y, z. The names which accompany the alphabet are: a, be, ce, che, de, e, efe, ge, hache, i, jota, ka, ele, elle, eme, ene, eñe, o, pe, cu, ere, erre, ese, te, u, ve, doble ve, equis, i griega, and zeta. Because Spanish grammar is similar to English grammar, the same method may be used to present parts of speech recognition. For example, "El gato es muy simpatico" is grammatically equivalent to "The cat is very nice" since the article is "el" (the), subject "gato" (cat), verb "es" (is), adverb "muy" (very), and adjective "simpatico" (nice).

It is important to note that the child needs to adjust to the masculine and feminine articles and reversing of nouns and adjectives.

For example "los gatos blancos" literally translated means "the cats white." The adjective follows the noun in the Spanish example but not in English. As you know, in English we would say "the white cats." This shouldn't be too confusing for the young child however, because his mind is at a stage when many languages can be readily learned without much difficulty.

KEEPING ALIVE A SENSE OF AWARENESS

Montessori felt that it was essential that the child, as small as he may be, understand how everything in nature is actually interrelated. She felt that if the child was cognizant of this, he would be a more thoughtful and considerate individual. We would see a human being who chooses to protect the environment rather than to destroy it. Because of the child's insight, he would make intelligent decisions about how best to preserve the beauty surrounding him.

He would treasure the sight of a squirrel scurrying up the side of a forest green pine tree on a crisp autumn morning. Or, while walking on the velvety sand at a nearby beach, he would watch with awe the seagulls gliding through the air and landing on the rocky shoreline a bit farther away. Appreciating this beauty, the child would think twice about littering the beautiful mountain ranges, beaches or deserts. Moreover, he would encourage his friends and relatives to do the same.

Take your child on as many excursions as possible. If you live near the coastline, take your child to different beaches so that he may make comparisons. First, take him to a beach where the water is a transparent blue and the sand and surrounding rocks are untouched by oil spills. Give your child plenty of freedom to analyze the different rocks and sea shells that he may find there. Devote some time to discussing the surrounding flora and fauna. Be sure to include the water cycle in your discussion. Your child will be fascinated to learn how water evaporates and is returned to us through rain clouds. Now that your child is older, he will also more fully appreciate a discussion about phytoplankton and the general food chain.

Next, visit a beach where there has been a recent oil spill. Discuss with your child how the oil not only spoils the beauty but interferes with the plant and aquatic life on this beach. Moreover, explain how the oil spill is damaging to the food chain.

These excursions help your child experience first hand all that nature has to offer him. By taking the time to answer his questions, you are encouraging him to be aware of

the world around him, and to better understand his place in the world.

Also keep in mind that in order for a child to reach his potential, he needs to be in an environment which will allow him to fully develop his own tendencies. This environment, wherever it may be, should include encouragement of expression rather than discouragement. Moreover, the child should feel a sense of security, coupled with love and approval.

This is not to say that the child has complete freedom to do as he pleases, rather, through a selected, prepared environment, the child learns successive tasks and skills, which will help him to relate and adjust to today's society. He is not pressured to learn a task or skill in a specified time frame. Rather, he is encouraged to absorb as much knowledge from each task as possible. Nor, is he led through understanding the task by a presenter. It is the child who makes the discoveries and spontaneous explosions associated with learning.

His requirements from us are simple. If we are to assist the child through this learning process, we must become more patient, respectful and giving. For it is only in this type of environment that true learning and a sense of fulfillment occur.

BIBLIOGRAPHY

Montessori, Maria, The Absorbant Mind
New York, New York, The Dell Publishing Co.
Inc., 1967.

Montessori, Maria, The Discovery of the Child
New York, New York, Ballatine Books, 1986.

Montessori, Maria, Dr. Montessori's Own Handbook.
New York, New York, Schoker Books, 1965.

Montessori, Maria, the Montessori Method.
Cambridge, Massachusetts, Robert Bentley,
Inc., 1965.

Montessori, Maria, The Secret of Childhood.
New York, New York, Ballatine Books, 1986.

Montessori, Maria, Spontaneous Activity in
Education. Cambridge, Massachusetts, Robert
Bentley, Inc., 1965.

SELECTED LIST OF ORGANIZATIONS

CANADIAN ALLIANCE OF HOME SCHOOLERS
195 Markville Road
Unionville, Ontario L3R 4VB
Canada
(416) 470-7930

This organization publishes a newsletter, Childs Play, which is read by many Canadian home educators. The newsletter is very well written and each issue is packed with useful information. In addition, the organization publishes books on homeschooling.

ALLIANCE FOR PARENTAL INVOLVEMENT
IN EDUCATION, INC.
P.O. Box 59
East Chatham, NY 12060-0059\

ALLPIE specializes in helping parents who wish to become involved in their children's education. This organization provides information to parents about public, private, and homeschooling. ALLPIE conducts workshops and conferences. For additional information write to the above address.

NORTH AMERICAN MONTESSORI TEACHERS'
ASSOCIATION
11424 Bellflower Blvd., N.E.
Cleveland, OH 44106

This organization offers a job listing service, publishes three issues of the NAMTA Journal per year, as well as other numerous services. Parents and teachers will want to write to obtain complete information about NAMTA.

MONTESSORI WORLD EDUCATIONAL INSTITUTE
P.O. Box 3808
San Luis Obispo, CA 93403

M.W.E.I. offers several services for interested parents and teachers. The organization offers workshops, inservice programs, and a list of books and Montessori materials which are available directly through the institute.

Appendix B
SELECTED RESOURCES FOR LESSON PLANNING

A BEKA BOOK
A Christian Textbook Ministry
118 St. John Street
Pensacola, FL 32523-9160

ABC SCHOOL SUPPLY, INC.
3312 N. Berkeley Lake Road
P.O. Box 10019
Duluth, GA 30136-9419
(404) 497-0001

ARISTOPLAY
Games for Fun and Learning
334 E. Washington Street
P.O. Box 7028
Ann Arbor, MI 48107
(313) 995-4353
(800) 634-7738

CABDEV INCORPORATED
Montessori Distributors Since 1972
3 Whitehorse Road, Unit 6
Downsview, Ontario MEJ 3G8 Canada

THE CANADIAN CHILDREN'S BOOK CENTRE
35 Spadina Road
Toronto, Ontario M5R 2S9 Canada
This organization is pleased to present information about Canadian
children's books, authors and illustrators.
Phone (416) 975-0010
FAX (416) 975-1839

EARLY WORK LEARNING TOOLS
P.O. Box 5635
Petaluma, CA 94953-5635

EDMUND SCIENTIFIC COMPANY
Supplier for science projects
11 East Gloucester Pine
Barrington, NJ 08007-1380

THE FIVE OWLS
2004 Sheridan Avenue South
Minneapolis, MN 55405
This journal gives an indepth coverage of what's happening in the world
of children's books.

GREY OWL INDIAN CRAFT MFG. CO.
113-15 Springfield Blvd.
Queens Village, NY 11429

HARPS OF LORIEN
Musical instruments for schools and homeschoolers
610 North Star Route
Questa, NM 87556

INDIAN STORE
Hobby City
1238 Beach Blvd.
Anaheim, CA 92804

IN-PRINT FOR CHILDREN
Supplies for Montessori matching exercises and more!
2113 Kenmore Avenue
Glenside, PA 19038

KINDERLINGS, INC.
Educational products for home and school use
978 Highland Circle
Los Altos, CA 94024

LADYBIRD BOOKS, INC.
49 Omni Circle
P.O. Box 1690
Auburn, ME 04210

LAKESHORE CURRICULUM MATERIALS COMPANY
2695 E. Dominguez Street
Carson, CA 90749

LEARNING MATERIALS WORKSHOP
58 Henry Street
Burlington, VT 05401

MONTESSORI WORLD EDUCATIONAL INSTITUTE
Supplier of Montessori apparatus and books
P.O. Box 3808
San Luis Obispo, CA 93403
(805) 541-3100

THE MONTESSORI ST. NICHOLAS
LEARNING MATERIALS
23-24 Princess Gate
London SW7-1PT
England

MUSEUM OF FINE ARTS BOSTON
465 Huntington Avenue
Boston, MA 02115
(617) 267-9300
Supplier of art postcards for matching picture exercises and
art appreciation exercises.

MUSIC FOR LITTLE PEOPLE
P.O. Box 1460
1144 Redway Drive
Redway, CA 95560
(707) 923-3991

SHAPES, INC.
8840 Rt. 36
P.O. Box 185
(800) 888-6580
(716) 335-6619
This company offers products for countless learning activities. The
products may be used for the many "home made" learning games
mentioned in this book. SHAPES, ETC. carries different maps in
various sizes, shapes of farm animals, oceanic life forms, and geometric
shapes to name a few.

THE UNIVERSITY PRINTS
21 East Street
P.O. Box 485
Winchester, MA 01890
This company offers a large selection of prints for student and teacher
use. The small 5-1/2" x 8" prints are great for the art appreciation and
matching picture exercises mentioned in this book.

USA TOY LIBRARY ASSOCIATION
2719 Broadway Avenue
Evanston, IL 60201
(708) 864-8240

VILLAGE FAIRE FOR EDUCATORS
10594 Combie Road #106515
Auburn, CA 95603
(916) 268-0607
This company offers Montessori classroom materials.

WARREN PUBLISHING HOUSE, INC.
Super Snack News
Totline Newsletter
P.O. Box 2250
Everett, WA 98203
(800) 334-4769
(206) 353-3100

YOUNG DISCOVERY LIBRARY
217 Main Street
Ossining, NY 10562
(914) 945-0600
The beautiful pictures found in the following titles will captivate the
preschooler as the parent or teacher reads the accompanying text.
ANIMALS IN WINTER
ANIMALS UNDERGROUND
BEARS, BIG AND LITTLE
THE BLUE PLANET: SEAS & OCEANS
ELEPHANTS: BIG, STRONG AND WISE
LIVING IN SOUTH AMERICA
LIVING WITH THE ESKIMOS
SEASHORE LIFE

To order "Montessori at Home" please send $10.95 plus
$1.50 for postage to:

American Montessori Consulting
P.O. Box 5062
Rossmoor, CA 90720-5062

INDEX